T0196959

Poems Through Life

A Journey Into the Soul

ASHLEY N. BURTON

authorHOUSE®

AuthorHouse™
1663 Liberty Drive
Bloomington, IN 47403
www.authorhouse.com
Phone: 1 (800) 839-8640

Published by AuthorHouse 12/08/2015

ISBN: 978-1-5049-6740-2 (sc)
ISBN: 978-1-5049-6739-6 (e)

Print information available on the last page.

This book is printed on acid-free paper.

Ashley Burton's Manuscript
for Poem Book Titile
Poems: Words for the Soul

Contents

I Feel a Fool

I've been beaten and put to show,
It's my own fault, yes I know,
For I was the one who played the game,
And now my virtue is put to shame,
It didn't go the first four times,
But fives the number that ruined my life,
For most a babe can bring happiness,
For me it's brought nothing but emptiness,
Yes, people love to shame me,
Tell me it's my fault and revel in my pain,
Not once have I denied my mistake,
Yet I'm trying to be responsible and right,
A fool I feel as my charade falls light,
The king will put this fool in the court yard stalks,
And I know this fool must sit and watch,
I must take the pain I put on my self,
This fool will join the laughs and belittle herself,
Depression ridden people see as a joke,
This little fool was a silly bloke,
To expect forgiveness from her one mistake,
This fool her life will pay everyday,
I feel i'm the fool,
And life has gone away.

Job Corps

I was there for a short time,
And while I was there I accomplished much,
I also had a great time,
I tried to follow some of the rules,
But when you're in the middle of nowhere,
The rules go to "somewhere",
I wasn't necessarily a good girl,
But I wasn't necessarily a bad girl,
I made my mistakes,
but i helped thousands of friends,
And that is why it was a great place.

Alone or Not Alone

I look at the stars,
I look at the ground,
I stop and listen,
All around,
I look at the stars,
A million there are,
Though they are very far,
I am farther,
I look at the ground,
It covers the earth round,
Many miles of ground,
I stand alone,
I look at the streams,
A few it seems,
They all run deep,
But I run upstream,
I look at the trees,
A thousand in the breeze,
in winter they freeze,
I am alone,
I look at the cells,

Where prisoners are held,
They all went to hell,
But I am the only one,
With a story to tell,
I look at the stars,
trees,
ground,
and streams,
It appears that I am alone.
But! In Greater aspect!
In greater measure!
Do I feel alone for my own pleasure,
Or am I simply amongst others?

You're Not At Fault

What do you do when the one you
love is afraid he'll hurt you,
And what do you do when you're so
afraid to loose someone close to you,
Can't you see the changes you bring on me,
Can't you see that i'm not who I use to be,
Put your trust in me,
Let your fears fly free,
Don't you know whatever happens to me,
Is meant to be,
And nothing is you fault.
I don't know how to breath
while my soul is on fire,
I don't know how to discard my desires,
It's raging in me and I wish I could
disbelieve my feelings,
Like you can do to me,
I know its hard for you,
I see it deep inside,
But can't you see,

Your fears I can subside.
Put your trust in me,
Let your fear fly free,
Don't you know whatever happens to me,
It's meant to be,
And nothing is your fault.
Their my choices, My influences,
And it's all on me, all on me,
Alll I ask is that you stay by me,
And as long as you are near,
Let your soul fly free,
Look at me,
You're not what's bad but good,
Hold on to me,
Keep me in your dreams,
And listen, listen to me,
You're not at fault.

Defect Butterfly

I started Off as a cute little caterpillar,
Big, fat, and round like a perfect Greece Pillar,
All the other little caterpillars don't like me much,
I'm not as smart as the rest of the bunch,
But deep in my millions of toes,
Deep in my little belly rolls,
I knew of a greater reason,
Why i was so diffrent and eager,
To grow.
So me and my friends clung on to each other,
Building our cocoons and making them better,
Once it was perfect,
We gathered inside,
My cocoon was close to sunshine,
But now Mother Nature is in control.
All the cocoons were safe and sound,
Except for the one that was far from the ground,
Mother Nature sent a giant staorm,
The Cocoon tumbled to the floor,
The storm raged and roared,
Then Suddenly calmed.
A few dents here and there,

certainly was a little rare,
No one ever thought that Butterfly
should be scared,
But that little Buttergly realized a change,
This would not be the same,
No longer a caterpillar, but a defect Butterfly.
All she could do was sit and cry,
My friends were fine,
Why wasn't I,
I counldn't fly,
My wings not working right,
Always rocking from side to side,
This little defect Butterly thought
she'd rather hide,
But the defect Butterfly flew far away,
Finding another defect Butterfly flying her way,
He told her to hang in there,
Pretty soon the Butterfly's will care,
With the help from her defect butterfly friend,
Her friends came back,
As she started life over again.

Lifes Decisions

Summers fillled with happiness and love,
Long winding walks,
Loved ones all around,
A faithful beginining,
I thought would never end.
Fall filled with blinded declines,
Happiness slowly fading,
Paths slowly taken,
Loved ones not so loving,
Minds change with the season.
Winter for an ending and beginning,
Loved one left me,
Snow covered the degrading leaves,
Happiness fell back to me,
Another path unwinding.
So it's Spring and the beginning
should be getting better,
What should be happy is depressing,
How I wish my first leaf in the Summer stayed,
How I wish minds didn't change,
I'm the only flower bloomed.

So Now it's my lifes decision,
Now it is my season,
I'm going to quit thinking of the first leaf,
for I know the first leaf has frozen,
Now I leave far far away,
To the place i'll be the most happiest,
To the place that will be Summer everyday.

Why?

I love my friends, Don't get me wrong,
And none of my ex's have ever been wrong,
But why do they think it's okay,
To hook up without knowing what I pray,
I still love my ex to this very day,
But I value your friendship so I say it's ok,
I hurt deep inside, I feel ashamed,
Cause I can't be honest and you're the blame,
This has happened to me too many times,
And now all I can say is,
"WHY?"

Happiest of All

Blackness, Darkness, Fear, Nothing,
Non-Existent to the human eye,
Using one of these words
creates nothing but a lie,
The happiest of all people live without these,
To become one, has the simplest means.
Light, Sunshine, Happiness, Hope Faith, Love,
Esxistent to everything and everyone,
To show all characteristics,
You achieved your goal.
Becomeng the happiest person,
You achieved all,
Becominng the happiest person,
You can not fall,
Not even death can take it away,
For death is just one step further,
Becoming the happiest of all.

How I See You

I wish I understood you more,
As I wade in your shallow pool,
Your walls of waves are way to high,
They crash, I'm thrown into the sky,
Now these clouds have me dreaming,
Your beautiful mystery has got me thinking,
And I'm scared our stars may never align.
I love your funny faces and glow frome the sun,
But you create tsunamis to destroy
who you've become,
I hope, young King Arthur that your
servants to your table come,
Come with spaghettie and carrot cake,
Cause I know you like them hun,
May you continually win your
battles in your games,
May you find another who loves anime.
May your dreams make and mold
you and bring you home to me,
I love you for you're nature and magic,
Don't let your tsunamis bring you tragic.

Come Close

Come Close to me,
I'll show the fire that I hide,
Rip my satin covering apart,
And show what's deep inside.
Come Close to me,
I swallowed the world,
See different cultures living,
See how they dance and twirl.
Come Close to me,
I've got paint spalashes upon my skin,
Each organ a different color,
No one knows where they begin.
Come Close to me,
See the round circle floating here,
Boys never get to hear it,
But men have developed ears.
Come Close to me,
See the liquid in this stove,
Boys lie to keep it iced,
While men stoke the coals.
Come Close to me,

For I have many things to show,
The deeper you travel with in me,
The more of me you'll know.
Come Close to me,
Do not be a boy,
But be a man,
Help my insides grow.

If Romeo Wasn't Loved

Why care?
Why bother?
Why compare me,
To a single flower?
Why beauty?
Why fair?
I do not care,
Vanity makes women,
Deceiful.
Why waste your breath?
Why waste my time?
I do not care,
For your silly rhyme.
Why silly boy?
Why would you die?
Do you not value,
Or pity your life?
Why me?
Why am I so special?
I am average,
I am an ordinary individual,

I've tried to make sense,
I've tried to make rhyme,
You make no sense,
You're wasting your time,
I have no love to give,
My heart not mine,
Why do you stay to fight?
A battle to die?
Don't waste your time.
So why care?
Why bother?
I am leaving you,
ROMEO RUN AWAY!
RUN FARTHER!!
GO HOME!!!

Leaving

So you two decided to take things slow,
Just in case the love runs cold,
And neither one believed it would work,
But you both hoped it would,
But only one believed it could.
You both understood what relationships need,
Though you both might have a different means,
Just for being together,
But you stilll went together.
For the first six months everything was great,
Each night she replayed her day in sleep,
Everything you said that was great,
She'd keep,
But what did you dream,
Probably not the same.
And after you lied to her when
she said it wouldn't work,
You really destroyed a great piece of work,
You had no reason to leave,
So you told a lie you thought was tactful,

Said that little girl wasn't active.
You thought she would stay while
you were moving on,
But deep down inside she was hurting,
So she decided she'd be moving,
All her hopes and dreams tossed aside,
She had to convince herself everything was a lie,
You didn't understand why she
thought you didn't love her,
But the lowest of lows was to lie
when you didn't want her,
Now she's found s a man who
loves having he raround,
But when that six month mark comes around,
She won't have that dream,
She won't ever think,
This man could be the one.
As soon as she does he will disappear,
And let's face it, we both know
she can't handle that fear,

so deep down inside she will go and hide,
Possibly maybe evern cry.
And it's a shame,
Because that women didn't mind,
That you played video games.
Some advice,
From one who is wise,
Don't say goodbye with a lie,
It will only tear the other one up inside,
If you don't feel the same anymore,
Just say so,
Instead of lying as you walk out the door.

Don't Cast Away

Sitting here playing magic with you,
Looking away,
Acting like i didn't notice you,
Your mom said stay,
I said if it's ok by you I may,
But you're not okay,
My heart burns with a fire of red,
My heart burns as you leave instead,
I'm acheing to stay,
But you're acheing to run away,
How can I show you I mean every word I say,
How can I show you I love you without you
Casting Me Away.

Car Crash

Car Crash has us both in a days,
Staying up talking late,
As we remember all those days,
I start to see why I feel for you in the first place,
We're laughing and were cryiing,
Oh no I am realizing,
You'll never love me in this way,
What do I do,
Do i love without you?
I guess I'll just go away.

Bar Night

Smoky room,
Country tunes,
Packed sardines,
Dancing moves,
A lonely girl,
One fight,
Tooo much trouble,
Went out for the night,
One male,
Drinking like a fish,
Looks at the girl,
Sees her wish,
Asks her to dance,
She politely accepts,
Secret face,
As they dance two step,
As the song ends,
Politness grows,
When she turns away,
Her pain shows,
She looks at her phone,

Blank as paper,
She wonders,
Does he know he matters?
On her mind from beginning to end,
It's too bad,
Stranger never had a chance,
She's still in love,
Even if he ain't,
Bar Night Rules,
Ladies and Fellas come to play,
And some,
Well, they come to get away.

Crazy

I love a man who can keep up the mystery,
But here lately,
Curiosity has me riddled crazy,
I feel likeI'm in the movie clue,
Who done it, Guess who?
But I feel as if you'll never tell me the end,
My hopes keep falling in,
You can tell me anything,
I'm not innocent just crazy,
Cause I'll neve leave you,
Even at the frustration of mystery,
And I'll never give up on you,
Cause I'm crazy about you,
Crazy and I love you.

Hollow Heart

Torment,
That's what i see when I look at you,
Love, could you,
Are you capable of such feelings.
Pain,
It's what I know you went through,
Hollow Hearts, they've found you,
Eat you're Soul, I swear they have,
Is that why darkness surrounds you?
Pithch Black,
The color of your aurau,
Red, Might replace the horror,
Could you open,
Open your heart,
Hollow,
I now see what is inside,
Love, I must fill it with love,
Maybe, then maybe you won't hide,
Could maybe then, You return love,
Please you hollow heart, let
me remake your soul,
Let me make our holllow heart grow.

Juliet Hates You

Feburary fourteenth,
How I Loathe the day,
Tow lovers come toghether,
And declared their love,
A Holiday.
I would rather celebrate,
My own reconciliation,
Then Celebrate another,
With the same Great Expectation.
Oh, St. Valentine,
How you love her,
We know how you have mourned,
But should we not,
Adore our own?
So come I say,
Lets celebrate our own reunion,
and let Feburary fourteenth,
Have it's own Communion.

Is it odd

Is it odd that i dream about you at night.
Is it odd that I see your face as bright,
Is it odd that i still have feelings for you,
Is it odd that my feelings are so true,
Is it odd that I keep this from you
Is it odd that i know you're not ready
Is it odd that I wish you'd be
Is it odd that i want you're heart to be mine,
Is it odd that i want our souls to intertwine,
Is it odd that I hide all of this from you,
Is it oddd that those precious
words i'll never speak to you.

Printed in the United States
By Bookmasters